12 THINGS TO KNOW ABOUT
SPACE EXPLORATION

by Rebecca Felix

12 STORY LIBRARY

www.12StoryLibrary.com

12-Story Library is an imprint of Peterson Publishing Company and Press Room Editions.

Produced for 12-Story Library by Red Line Editorial

Photographs ©: John Raoux/AP Images, cover, 1; NASA, 4, 6, 7, 9, 10, 11, 15, 20, 24, 25, 29; Shutterstock Images, 5, 16, 22; Mars One/Brian Versteeg/AP Images, 12, 29; Robert Cohen/AP Images, 13; NASA/Ames/SETI Institute/JPL-Caltech, 14; Paulo Afonso/ Shutterstock Images, 17; Sunset Boulevard/Corbis, 18; Tomas Mikula/Shutterstock Images, 21; Tatsuo Nakajima/AP Images, 23; Reed Saxon/AP Images, 26, 27

ISBN
978-1-63235-032-9 (hardcover)
978-1-63235-092-3 (paperback)
978-1-62143-073-5 (hosted ebook)

Library of Congress Control Number: 2014946808

Printed in the United States of America
Mankato, MN
October, 2014

12 STORY LIBRARY

Go beyond the book. Get free, up-to-date content on this topic at 12StoryLibrary.com.

TABLE OF CONTENTS

1

THE SPACE AGE BEGAN MORE THAN 50 YEARS AGO

On October 4, 1957, the Soviet Union (now Russia) launched Sputnik 1. Sputnik was the first manmade satellite. Though only the size of a beach ball, the little satellite made a big impact. It started a Space Age that has lasted more than 50 years. Some scientists and historians argue the Space Age is over. However, others say recent innovations and projects show the era of space exploration is still alive and well.

At the beginning of the Space Age, there was a Space Race. The Soviet Union and the United States raced to be the first to launch people into space, land an astronaut on the moon, and explore space. On May 25, 1961, President

1,400
Number of Earth orbits the first spacecraft, Sputnik 1, completed in 1958.

- The Space Age started in 1957 when Russia launched the satellite Sputnik.
- On July 20, 1969, Neil Armstrong became the first person to stand on the moon.
- Space exploration still excites people in the United States and around the world.

A photo of Earth taken by the *Apollo 16* crew in 1972

NASA's facilities on Cape Canaveral in Florida

THINK ABOUT IT

How would you help make sure space exploration continues? Would you give up your time to campaign? Would you donate your own money?

John F. Kennedy announced his goal of sending an American to the moon before 1970. The National Aeronautics and Space Administration (NASA) would be in charge of the US space program. Over the next eight years, NASA scientists worked hard to develop technology that could safely land an astronaut on the moon. On July 20, 1969, Kennedy's goal was achieved. That day, astronaut Neil Armstrong stepped off the ladder of *Apollo 11*'s lunar module and onto the surface on the moon.

Since 1969, NASA's missions have launched satellites, telescopes, research vehicles, and astronauts into space. In 2011, NASA announced the end of its space shuttle program that transported astronauts into space and to the International Space Station. But that did not mean Americans no longer could explore space. Instead of racing against each other, Russia, the United States, and other spacefaring countries now work together. American astronauts travel to space in Russian spacecraft. Private companies in the United States are also developing their own spacefaring vessels. The exploration of space continues to excite scientists, Americans, and people around the globe.

THE SPACE STATION REMAINS IMPORTANT

The International Space Station (ISS) was launched in 1998. It has orbited Earth ever since. The ISS circles Earth more than 15 times a day. It follows the same loop, never going anywhere new. But many believe the ISS is important to future exploration.

The ISS is maintained by astronauts from many different countries, including the United States, Russia, and China. The astronauts spend months at a time on the ISS. While on board, they perform tests and do maintenance. The ISS is also used as a research lab for gravity and space experiments. Astronauts research the effects that zero gravity has on living beings. Zero gravity is a state of being weightless. To understand these effects, the ISS crew studies rats that live onboard.

Many hope the ISS has a long future.

INSIDE THE ISS

The ISS is approximately the size of a football field. Huge solar panel wings provide power to the station. The ISS has more living space than a typical six-bedroom house does. Astronauts use a huge bay window to see approaching spacecraft, the moon, stars, and Earth. They can also see a sunrise or sunset every 45 minutes.

Astronaut Susan J. Helms looks out a window on the ISS.

The ISS also shows what can happen to spacecraft long-term. Zero gravity can cause dust to clog filters. Bacteria behave differently when in space. They grow in strange formations and weigh more than bacteria on Earth. These small problems could become major ones on a future trip to Mars. Mars is millions of miles away. Crews could not turn around or get new supplies. Solving these issues on the ISS may make reaching new and distant destinations possible.

In 2013, President Barack Obama extended the ISS's orbit to at least 2024. It will continue to be important in space exploration.

15
Number of countries that have been involved in the ISS.

- The ISS orbits Earth more than 15 times each day.
- Although it does not travel new places, the experiments onboard the ISS are important to future exploration.
- Rats live onboard permanently, while humans visit for months at a time.
- Research onboard the ISS could make long-distance space missions possible.

3

AN ASTRONAUT WILL LIVE IN SPACE FOR ONE YEAR

Mark and Scott Kelly are 50-year-old identical twins. Both are astronauts. Mark is retired, but Scott is still an active astronaut. Scott once stayed on the ISS for six months. The longest human stay on the ISS lasted seven months. Scott is looking to beat this record in the name of science. He will stay on board the ISS for one year. NASA can study how space affects him in that time.

Scott and Mark have the same genetics. Scott will be studied and tested in space. On Earth Mark will also be studied and tested. Their health will be compared before, during, and after the experiment. Their minds and their immune and other body systems will be tested. Changes in aging and in their

blood, feces, and vision will also be studied. Scott even volunteered to have sensors drilled into his head to monitor his vision. NASA said this was not needed.

3
Number of missions Scott Kelly completed between 1999 and 2011.

- Staying in space for long periods of time affects the human body and mind.
- Scott Kelly will be studied onboard the ISS for one year. His identical twin Mark will be studied on Earth.
- How space affects Scott over one year will help NASA prepare for a future manned Mars mission.

Astronaut Scott Kelly aboard the *Discovery* in 2010

WHAT HAPPENS TO HUMANS IN SPACE?

Being in space a short period of time has effects, too. Astronauts may experience headaches from blood circulating differently. Some also feel dizzy. Astronauts do not need to walk or lift anything in space. That means they might lose muscle mass. They can also lose bone mass. Lost bone mass cannot be regained. Exposure to higher amounts of radiation in space can cause cancer or brain damage.

The goal is to see what could happen to humans in space over a long period of time. The effects of long-term space exposure will help NASA prepare astronauts for future missions to faraway destinations such as Mars.

4

NASA MAY SEND ASTRONAUTS TO MARS

Mars has long fascinated people. It has many similarities to Earth. It has seasons. It also has 24-hour days and polar ice caps. There is evidence that water in liquid form was once on Mars. Where there is water, there could be some type of life.

No person has ever landed on Mars. NASA has done flybys. It has sent orbiters to capture photographs. Since the 1970s, 18 spacecraft have been launched by many nations to land on Mars. Only eight were successful. The others got lost, crashed, or missed the planet.

Many scientists hope to learn if there is life on Mars.

35 million

Distance from Earth, in miles, when Mars gets closest to Earth.

- Mars is very far from Earth and difficult to land on.
- Eighteen spacecraft have been launched to land on Mars since the 1970s.
- Only eight of those landed successfully.
- NASA is planning to land astronauts on Mars in the 2030s.

Mars rover *Opportunity* took an image of itself in 2004.

Mars's unpredictable atmosphere makes it a difficult planet to land on. Winds and dust storms can change how dense the atmosphere is. Its distance from Earth makes it difficult to visit, too.

Mars's distance from Earth changes by millions of miles during the year. On average it is about 140 million miles (225 million km) away. The fastest available spacecraft would take months to reach it. A return flight means astronauts would be in space twice as long. This can pose health risks.

Though there are challenges, NASA is planning a manned mission to Mars for the 2030s. It will send an empty spacecraft in 2017 as a test. Not everyone thinks a Mars mission is a good idea. Some people think it is not possible. But its supporters disagree. They think being first to land on Mars will inspire further space exploration.

5

FOUR PEOPLE MAY LIVE ON MARS BY 2025

Mars One is a private company in the Netherlands. It plans to send humans to live on Mars. In the spring of 2014, more than 200,000 people had applied. Mars One narrowed them down to approximately 1,000 applicants.

It will continue to do so until four people are left. Those four people will train for eight years. In 2024, they will leave for their new home. They will never return to Earth. Their flight will last seven to eight months.

FINDING WATER, FOOD, AND AIR ON MARS

As the first Mars One group prepares for its journey, a rover and cargo loads will land on Mars. The rover will build living pods. It will begin gathering Martian soil and the ice beneath it. It will set up a system to extract water from the ice. Then, it will extract oxygen from the water. Humans will take over when they land. They will also grow plants without soil for food.

An artist's concept of what a Mars One colony may look like

3

Hours of daily exercise Mars One will require of crewmembers during their journey to Mars.

- Mars One is a private company that wants to start a colony on Mars.
- People chosen to live on Mars will train for eight years before leaving.
- They will never return to Earth.
- Cargo loads will take building materials to the planet.
- Mars One has plans for technology that will set up living pods and make food production and breathing possible.

Mars One will then select and train four others. They will send them to Mars two years after the first group. The company hopes to continue this pattern until a colony of people lives on Mars.

Mars One will send rovers to the planet before the people arrive. The rovers will build pods where

THINK ABOUT IT

Would you want to live on Mars? What if you could never return to Earth? How would your life be different on Mars than it is now? Write a paragraph to explain your answer.

the Mars One participants will live. They will create a system to make water and breathable air.

Mars One's mission has received much criticism. Critics think living on Mars is impossible. Astronaut Buzz Aldrin believes Mars One's timeline is not attainable. But Mars One believes its mission will be successful.

Maggie Duckworth from Missouri hopes to be picked for a Mars One mission.

EARTH'S "TWIN" HAS BEEN DISCOVERED

In April 2014, NASA's Kepler Space Telescope spotted an exoplanet. It was named Kepler-186f. Scientists think there are thousands of exoplanets. But Kepler-186f is the first one found that is similar to Earth. Kepler-186f is close in size to Earth. It is also in the habitable zone of its star, just like Earth is to its star, the sun.

But scientists say being similar to Earth and in a habitable zone does not guarantee the planet is actually habitable. The environment and atmosphere could make the planet unfit for living things.

Some scientists believe Kepler-186f may look similar to this illustration.

THINK ABOUT IT

Do you think there are other planets very similar to Earth in the galaxy? Do you think any have life? Use your imagination. In what ways could this life be similar? How could it be different?

490

Distance in light years between Earth and Kepler-186f.

- NASA discovered an exoplanet very similar to Earth.
- Some scientists are calling Kepler-186f Earth's twin or cousin.
- The discovery of Kepler-186f proves any star could have planets orbiting it that are able to support life.

Some scientists believe Kepler-186f is more like Earth's cousin. They say this because it is not identical to Earth. It orbits its star once every 130 days. That is less than half as long as Earth's one-year orbit around the sun. It is also a bit darker and colder than Earth. Currently, there is no way to visit Kepler-186f to find out if it has life. It is so far away it would take thousands of years to reach.

Kepler-186f's existence alone is exciting and important. Finding it suggests there could billions more habitable exoplanets orbiting the stars.

A photo of the sun rising over Earth taken from the *Endeavor* space shuttle

ALIEN LIFE COULD BE FOUND WITHIN 20 YEARS

All kinds of aliens appear in movies, books, and TV shows. In real life, scientists search for microorganisms within Earth's solar system. And many think intelligent life may exist outside it. Two scientists say astronomers will find out for sure soon. They estimate alien life will be found within 20 years if money is invested in the technology to identify it.

Seth Shostak and Dan Werthimer are Search for Extraterrestrial Intelligence (SETI) Institute scientists. In May 2014, they met with the House Committee on Science, Space, and Technology in Washington, DC. They discussed searching for alien life. The SETI scientists said estimates claim at least 70 percent of all stars have planets orbiting them. There may be tens of billions of planets in Earth's galaxy. With so many possible planets out there, Werthimer said, "It would be bizarre if we are alone."

Alien life forms may look more like bacteria than little green people.

THINK ABOUT IT

Do you think alien life exists? Why or why not? Find articles or research online to support your opinion.

150 billion

Number of known galaxies in the universe.

- People have searched for aliens for more than 50 years.
- Alien life could be in the form of microbes in our solar system or intelligent life beyond it.
- Some scientists say it would be odd if Earth is the only planet with life.

ALIEN LIFE INVESTIGATIONS

The belief in the possibility of alien life in space dates back to ancient Greece. Throughout the centuries, people continued to study and form theories about it. During the Space Age in the 1950s, people began to actually look for aliens. SETI Institute formed in the 1960s. Alien sightings have been reported by people ever since. None have ever been scientifically confirmed.

The telescopes at SETI's Hat Creek Allen Telescope Array are nearly 20 feet (6 m) in diameter.

WARP DRIVE AND INTERSTELLAR TRAVEL CREATE DEBATE

Interstellar travel is traveling to and between stars. The closest star to Earth is 24 trillion miles (39 trillion km) away. Even the fastest spacecraft would take 17,000 years to reach it.

Warp speed is the idea of traveling faster than the speed of light. The speed of light is the fastest known speed. At the speed of light, it would take one second to travel around our planet seven and a half times. For years, warp speed has been science fiction. Using warp drive for interstellar travel has been part of many books, movies, and TV shows about space. But most people believe it is not possible in real life.

Recently NASA engineers announced they are working on developing warp drive technology. They plan to form a warp bubble around a spacecraft. The bubble would be able to alter time. The time within the bubble would be different from the time outside it. This would allow

THE SPEED OF LIGHT AND LIGHT YEARS

The speed of light is 186,282 miles (299,729 km) per second. How far light travels in one year is called a light year. The closer a lighted object is, the faster people see it. Moonlight travels to our eyes in just over one second. Sunlight takes eight minutes. Starlight takes years. Some stars are billions of light years away.

The starship on the TV show *Star Trek* used warp drive to travel through space.

1,600

Hours it took NASA scientists to develop a concept for a faster-than-light starship.

- Interstellar travel is not possible as the closest star is thousands of light years away.
- Warp drive is traveling faster than light, and it would make interstellar travel possible.
- NASA is working on creating a spacecraft that travels at warp speed.
- Critics of warp speed believe the technology is not possible to create.

interstellar travel to take months or weeks rather than thousands of years.

Some critics believe spending time and money on warp drive and interstellar travel is a waste. But some astronomers believe that although these things are not possible yet, they could be in the future if research continues.

ASTRONAUTS CAN PRINT 3-D TOOLS IN SPACE

Space explorers on the TV show *Star Trek: The Next Generation* used a replicator. It was a machine that created exact copies of tools, clothes, and foods. When the show aired in the early 1990s, replicators were science fiction. But in summer 2014, a similar machine became a reality.

Made In Space is a US company. It created a 3-D printer to be used in space. 3-D printers are robotic machines. They make items and tools from materials such as plastic and metals. They print items layer by layer from a computer file. The Made In Space 3-D printer will do the same thing. But it will work in zero gravity. New parts or tools are impossible to send to a spacecraft

Scientists on the ISS will soon use a 3-D printer in their laboratory.

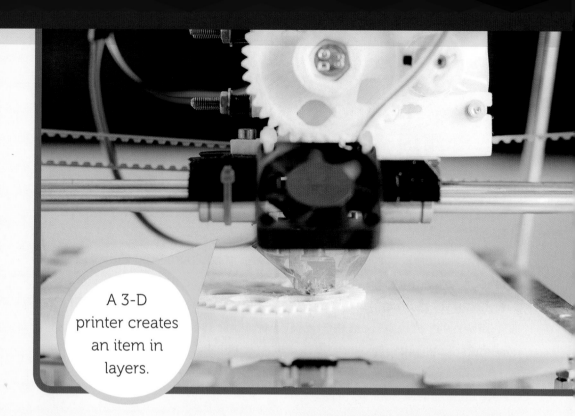

A 3-D printer creates an item in layers.

traveling months or years into space. The 3-D printer would solve this problem. It would help make longer trips possible. It may also make exploration cheaper. It would eliminate the need for many cargo trips to the ISS.

Made In Space's printer was launched to the ISS in September 2014. It will print a series of items onboard as a test. NASA and Made In Space hope to install a larger, permanent 3-D printer on the ISS by 2015. They hope other space companies will pay to have satellites built onboard that could then be launched right from the ISS.

1
Number of 3-D printers launched to the ISS in 2014.

- Made In Space created a 3-D printer to print items in space.
- Printing tools and parts aboard spacecraft would make exploration more efficient, safer, and cheaper.
- NASA and Made In Space hope to install a permanent 3-D printer on the ISS that could build satellites.

ASTRONAUTS WILL USE MOBILE APPS IN SPACEFLIGHT

Since the end of the US space shuttle program, Russian spacecraft have taken US astronauts to the ISS. These flights have cost the US hundreds of millions of dollars. In 2012, NASA gave contracts to three private companies: Boeing, SpaceX, and Sierra Nevada Corporation. Each is to build a spacecraft by 2017 to transport astronauts to the ISS. The companies are trying to make efficient, updated spacecraft.

Boeing has partnered with mobile technology company Samsung. They are creating cool apps and technology for the Boeing CST-100 spacecraft.

Some apps are already used onboard the ISS. Its low orbit allows the station to have a Wi-Fi connection. One onboard app is World Map. It can be set to alert astronauts when the ISS orbits over

Astronauts may soon be able to use apps while traveling to the ISS.

certain parts of the world. Samsung and Boeing will make this app available during the flight to the ISS as well. There are several in-flight apps the companies have planned for the CST-100. Some might help astronauts monitor spacecraft equipment. Others may let astronauts take photos and share them with family and friends during the flight. The CST-100 also has wireless touchscreen control panels. Samsung tablets will be installed overhead for crew members.

6

Number of planned in-flight apps Boeing and Samsung will make available on the CST-100.

- US astronauts have relied on Russian spacecraft to fly them to the ISS since the end of the US space shuttle program.
- NASA contracted three US companies to create spacecraft that can fly astronauts to the ISS.
- Boeing partnered with Samsung to install tablets and make apps available during flights to the ISS on their spacecraft.

The CST-100 is Boeing's first spacecraft.

BOEING

7 PERSON MAX CAPACITY

4 PERSON MAX LOAD

THE FIRST FLYBY OF PLUTO WILL HAPPEN IN 2015

Pluto is in a part of the solar system called the Kuiper Belt. It is 4.7 billion miles (7.6 billion km) from Earth. No spacecraft has ever landed on or flown directly past Pluto. In 2006, NASA launched a flyby mission to take photos of Pluto. The spacecraft, New Horizons, is one of the fastest spacecraft ever. But even it will take nearly ten years to reach Pluto. It will be the first flyby of an unexplored planet in more than 30 years—if scientists agree to call Pluto a planet again.

Pluto was considered a planet for more than 70 years. The International Astronomical Union (IAU) gives space objects their scientific names. In 2006, the IAU determined Pluto was a "dwarf planet." It has five moons. One of them, Charon, is nearly as big as Pluto. It is sometimes also called Pluto-Charon, or a "double planet."

Some scientists still argue Pluto is a planet. Many think the 2015 flyby and the photos that come from it may open the debate again. After examining Pluto, New Horizons will move deeper into the Kuiper Belt to study other objects.

The Hubble Space Telescope took the first image of Pluto in 1994.

THE KUIPER BELT

Some scientists believe the icy, rocky objects in the Kuiper Belt may be made of the material that formed the planets. They believe the objects may have stopped joining and growing long ago. Studying them may give scientists clues about the history of the solar system.

1 trillion
Estimated number of comets in the Kuiper Belt.

- NASA's New Horizons spacecraft will fly by Pluto in 2015.
- It will be the first flyby to a new planet in more than 20 years.
- In 2006, Pluto was determined to be a dwarf planet rather than a planet.
- Some scientists still think Pluto is a planet and hope the discoveries made by the flyby will help open the debate again.

The Kuiper Belt contains many rocky objects, such as this one.

SPACE TOURISM MAY BECOME A REALITY

Since 1961, more than 500 people have traveled to space. Only a few have not been astronauts. But as of June 2014, more than 700 tourists had plans for space travel. Aerospace company Virgin Galactic has been selling spaceflight tickets since 2004. Each ticket costs $250,000. Several celebrities have reportedly bought one. They include singers Justin Bieber and Katy Perry and actor Ashton Kutcher.

The Virgin Galactic SpaceShipTwo at its hangar in the Mojave Desert in California in 2013

300 of Virgin Galactic's customers are briefed on the company's progress.

Virgin Galactic has prepared flight plans and training programs. But people may never get the chance to cash in their tickets. Some space enthusiasts think the company will never be ready to send people into space. Each year since 1999, the company has announced commercial spaceflight is just one to three years away. The company has completed successful test flights. But it still has not flown people into space. Some progress has been made, though. In May 2014, the Federal Aviation Administration granted the company flight approval. Spaceport America in southern New Mexico is a giant airport built for spacecraft. It is ready for Virgin Galactic to move in.

Its hangars are empty for now. But they may be filled in the near future. Many other companies have plans to send tourists into space one day.

68

Altitude, in miles, at which the Virgin Galactic spaceflight will fly.

- Virgin Galactic has been selling tickets for space travel since 2004.
- More than 700 people have reserved tickets.
- Spaceport America is a spacecraft airport in New Mexico.

FACT SHEET

- A solar system is a group of planets orbiting a star. Earth's solar system orbits the sun, which is a star. It consists of eight planets—nine when Pluto was considered a planet. Earth's solar system is made up of three zones. Mercury, Venus, Earth, and Mars are the inner, rocky planets. The next zone is made up of Jupiter, Saturn, Uranus, and Neptune. These planets are giant and made up of gas. The third zone is the Kuiper Belt. It consists of Pluto and its moons and billions of icy masses.

- Space exploration began in 1957. That year the Soviet Union launched the first satellite, Sputnik I. The first US satellite was launched a year later. The Space Age had begun. It lasted more than 50 years. The United States and the Soviet Union (now Russia) have long competed to be the first to complete landmark space exploration missions.

- The first person in space was Russian astronaut Yuri Gagarin in 1961. American astronauts Neil Armstrong and Buzz Aldrin were the first people to land on the moon in 1969. Since 1961, more than 500 people have traveled into space. The International Space Station was launched in 1998 and has orbited the earth ever since.

- In August 2012, a NASA probe left our solar system and began interstellar travel. Some scientists dream of sending spacecraft deep into other galaxies in interstellar travel using warp drive to travel faster than the speed of light. It is an idea that has long been present in science fiction but may not be a real possibility.

GLOSSARY

budget
A plan for how much money can be spent and on what.

cargo
Goods carried on a ship, plane, or spacecraft.

commercial
Suitable for a public audience.

exoplanet
A planet that orbits a star other than the sun.

flybys
Flights of spacecraft past a planet, moon, or other space object.

galaxy
Any one of the large groups of planets and stars that make up the universe.

gravity
The force that pulls or makes things fall toward Earth.

habitable
Safe and fit for people to live in.

microorganisms
Small, brainless organisms that can only be seen with a microscope.

monitor
To continually check something over a certain period of time.

orbit
To travel in a circular path around an object such as the sun or a planet.

satellites
Spacecraft sent into space to orbit a planet, the sun, or a moon.

FOR MORE INFORMATION

Books

Bingham, Caroline. *First Space Encyclopedia*. New York: Dorling Kindersley, 2008. Print.

Goldsmith, Mike. *Space*. New York: Kingfisher, 2012. Print.

Stott, Carole. *Space Exploration*. New York: Dorling Kindersley, 2010. Print.

Websites

Amazing Space
www.amazing-space.stsci.edu/resources/explorations

KidAstronomy.com
www.kidsastronomy.com

NASA Education
www.nasa.gov/audience/forstudents/k-4

The Sky: Space Exploration
www.seasky.org/space-exploration.html

INDEX

About the Author

Rebecca Felix is a writer and editor from Minnesota. She has written and edited books for kids on all kinds of topics. These include fairy tales, manners, states, animals, weather, and space.